MY IDENTITY
AND OTHER POEMS

LUTHER WHITLEY

authorHOUSE®

AuthorHouse™
1663 Liberty Drive
Bloomington, IN 47403
www.authorhouse.com
Phone: 1 (800) 839-8640

Published by AuthorHouse 07/08/2020

ISBN: 978-1-7283-6516-9 (sc)
ISBN: 978-1-7283-6515-2 (e)

Library of Congress Control Number: 2020911534

Print information available on the last page.

Any people depicted in stock imagery provided by Getty Images are models, and such images are being used for illustrative purposes only.
Certain stock imagery © Getty Images.

Cover design by Jada Mitchell

This book is printed on acid-free paper.

What is poetry? Poetry is beautiful living words that when uttered can be seen as well as heard.

-Luther Whitley

CONTENTS

ACKNOWLEDGEMENTS

Other than the Almighty, no one can I thank more than Jada Mitchell for helping me to complete this book of poems. Besides coming up with the cover design for "My Identity," Jada did almost everything else. Since I don't type, she was my transcriber. She had to try to make sense of what sometimes didn't make sense. For someone not long out of high school, Jada was well equipped for the job.

To measure what she was against, consider that I have no computer, nor am I tech savvy. This meant that everything had to be communicated over the phone (which I am not good with) or in person. Adding to the complexity is that more poems kept coming to me, asking that they be included in the book (One such poem is found on page 14). I must have told Jada a dozen times that we were finished. She was patient with me, took it all in stride.

That horrible Corona pandemic was, in a way, beneficial for us (I won't say blessing in disguise) in that it kept Jada home from work three days a week giving her time to help me. I cannot thank her enough.

INTRODUCTION

The poem "My Identity," hence the title of the book, was inspired by Mahmoud Darwish's poem, "Identity Card." While Darwish suffers because of not having an identity card, "My Identity," is based on a totally different identity problem as is shown in the poem's surprise ending. The other poems found in this book run the gamut, from religion to love and marriage.

Some of the poems included in this book will make you think as well as make you blink. There are poems about exciting people, places, and things. There are poems that are sometimes serious, sometimes humorous, sometimes satirical, sometimes even educational. My favorite is Retirement-Nothing to Do. Probably because I am a retiree with plenty to do.

While the book is directed primarily to adults and young adults, there is a section that focuses on children, Section 10. I tried to make it a point to offer helpful and practical suggestions to children.

Luther Whitley

SECTION 1: PEOPLE

The word "people" has a number of definitions, including human beings, as distinct from lower animals or inanimate things; while people, human beings are lauded for their comparatively big brains and big intellect, people fail miserably when it comes to getting along with one another. Many have little or no respect for their Creator. Fewer and fewer are like wise King David who wrote: "Know ye that the Lord He is God: It is he that hath made us and not we ourselves." -Psalms 100:3 KJV

MORNING PEOPLE

Morning people, Morning people

Soldiers and farmers are among those who believe in getting an early morning start

Morning People

On the farm it was the rooster that told the farmer when it was time to get up, usually around 4 or 5 a.m.

It was the bugle's reveille that told the soldiers to "rise and shine," "Up and at'm"

It was the claim of the U.S. Army that its people, like the rooster got more work done by 9 a.m. than most folks did all day long

Did this mean that morning people were more industrious than others?

Not necessarily, there are a lot of people who get a lot done after the sun goes down

Night people, Night people

ALL YOU CAN EAT

When he walked away from the buffet line
His plate like a shovel carried a mountain of food
Which, judging from his girth, he was sure to eat
And so, along with the turkey and dressing
He devoured the mashed potatoes and gravy
There was also the meatloaf and gravy
He consumed the collard greens and yams
Took in a huge helping of macaroni and cheese
All the while partaking of a side dish of seafood salad
Included in this frenzy was a big piece of cornbread
And not to be overlooked were those six chicken wings
After that there was the huge slice of apple pie
Topped with several scoops of vanilla ice cream
After a piece of that luscious Devil's food cake
And after 6 more chicken wings
he boldly asked if there were any diet sodas.

THE RICH AND FAMOUS-ARE THEY REALLY LIVING?

There are those who have a great quantity
Of valuable material possessions.
They have stocks and bonds, money in
banks, fine homes, fine clothes, as well as fine cars
Those are the rich, but are they really living?
Others have done great things and so have
made the who's who list thus their names
and faces are instantly recognized by many people
in many places.
These are the famous, but are they really living?
Consider what some of these two groups have to endure
Some of the rich and famous live in constant fear,
fear of kidnapping, robbery, and or extortion
Some are hounded by the paparazzi who sometimes
camp outside of their homes
Some of the rich and famous feel that this goes
with the territory
Others, on the other hand, severely loath these
dog-like snoops
And so, they don disguises or sneak around
when they go out
Again, we ask, are they really living?
From the rooftop of his Manhattan apartment, Mr. Rich
is able to helicopter to the airport
where his personal Lear jet awaits to

whisk him to almost any place on earth
Like a migrating bird, in a matter of hours
he may have gone from a cold New York winter
to basking in the warm sunshine
of the French Riviera
Whether he stays in his own chalet in Nice
or Monaco or whether it's a five-star hotel,
a multitude of servants are at his
beck and call
It seems that such a person wants for nothing
He never has to ask what something cost
because he can always afford it
Such a person is thought of by many
as really living
Such a life is thought of by many
as the real life
But guess what?
They are not really living!
Do you know why?
They are still in this world
And no one in this world is really living
No one in this world has gotten hold of the real life
Even if you know the truth and the truth has set you free
Even if you are in this world but no part of it
Even if you have no love for this world or the things in it
You are all still in this world You are still in this life
Not until this world is done away with
Not until this earth becomes a paradise
as God intended
Not until the benefits of Christ's ransom sacrifice

will have been applied to those living in that paradise

Not until sickness, disease, and death have been done away with

Not until pain and suffering are things of the past

Not until the countless millions in the grave are resurrected

Not until all these things happen will anyone have gotten hold of the real life

So whether we suffer abject poverty or whether we are filthy rich

If we are still in this world

If we are still in this life

Then we are not really living We merely exist

KIND AND LOVING PEOPLE GIVE GIFTS

Kind and loving people practice gift giving
Kind and loving people don't exchange gifts
Kind and loving people know that exchanging
is not truly giving but trading
Kind and loving people give without looking
for something in return

LARRY'S JOHN

There is a toilet in Minneapolis
Where many people now go
Not because they have to go, or
need to go, but because they want to go
They want to see the stool on
which Larry sat
See the floor on which his feet he pat
They want to see that partition
under which he allowed his hand to roam
Hoping for another hand to join his own
This toilet, they feel they just have to see
It's Larry's John, the toilet
that will live in infamy

MAINTAIN

A friend I once had
who spent his time maintaining
Unlike so many others who spent their time constantly complaining
Because "maintaining" was always his response
Folks took to calling him maintain
For no matter how grim things look
He was never heard to complain
Jovial and effervescent is how he always was
Bright and witty was he too
Ask him how he was fairing, standard answer:
"Maintaining, that's all we can do."

MY IDENTITY

(Inspired by Mahomoud Darwish)

A black man I am
And I have a job
A decent and well-paying job
I have a wife and two children
We were planning to buy a house next year
Do I have cause to be angry?
A black man I am
And I have a job
Operating an asphalt paving machine
Trucks dump their loads into my machine
Which spreads the asphalt evenly to make a road
I have a wife and two children
I can clothe and feed them
As well as to save for a house
From the black top I spread
I never apply for benefits that I don't qualify for
Don't cheat on my taxes
Do I have cause to be angry?
A black man I am
And I have a job No fancy title do I own
Patient in a country where racism
Is still alive and kicking even if not as high
As it once did
Traced my roots
Took me back to Alabama
Before civil rights were accorded blacks

Before we were allowed across the tracks
Before discrimination was illegal
My father was from those who lived off the land
A sharecropper was he
And my grandfather, the son of a runaway slave
Was a sharecropper too
I once lived in a house without plumbing
It was generally referred to as a shack
Does my ancestry define me?
It tells only where I came from
What's there to be angry about?
A black man I am
And I have a job
My height: Six feet one
Weight: Two hundred pounds
Hair color: Black
Color of eyes: Brown
My most distinguishing feature:
A warm and friendly smile I've been told,
Disarming anyone reluctant to approach me
My address:
I live in a two-bedroom apartment
Where my two daughters share a room
We have been saving up to buy a house
Do I have to cause to be angry?
A black man I am
And I have a job
But I am also angry, very, very angry
What do I have to be angry about?
Have I been discriminated against?

Racially profiled?
Have I been mugged?
Have my wife and daughters been violated?
Has my home been broken into?
Something just as bad
My life savings are gone
And even worse, I am now $300,000 in debt
Why? I'll tell you why!
Because somebody's been impersonating me
Yes, my identity has been stolen

BEAUTIFUL PEOPLE

A fabulous physique
makes not a beautiful person
A grille of 32 pretty, pearly whites
makes not a beautiful person
Hair that is given all the needed care
makes not a beautiful person
Eyes that literally hypnotize
makes not a beautiful person
What then makes a truly beautiful person?
It is what one is on the inside
Possessing and displaying the fruits
of the spirit is what shows one to be
truly beautiful, and they are:
Love, joy, peace, patience, kindness, goodness,
faith, mildness, and self-control
Possessing these and displaying them
is what makes beautiful people

ARMED AND DANGEROUS

I was not a soldier, sailor, airman or marine
but I was armed and dangerous
I was not a policeman, FBI or Secret Service
but I was armed and dangerous
I was not a criminal, drug dealer or thug
but I was armed and dangerous
I practiced no martial arts
but I was armed and dangerous
I was well liked and welcomed by most people
but I was armed and dangerous
I could be seen daily going from house to house
but I was armed and dangerous
I kept in my truck two big sticks, one baseball bat
and my favorite, a huge table leg
One of these I carried at all times,
that is how I was armed and dangerous
I never ran from dogs but to them
because I was armed and dangerous,
Whenever a dog would bolt and run to me
I would take off running to him
because I was armed and dangerous
I once chased a Rottweiler two blocks
before giving up the chase
Knocked a pitbull silly with my
Louiseville Slugger when he
jumped the fence to get to me

You see, I was armed and dangerous
I never attacked a dog without provocation
even though I was armed and dangerous
Of course, provocation could be a menacing
bark or growl
That's why I was armed and dangerous
I always believed that your pet was your pet
and if you wanted to keep your pet
then you should keep your pet away from me
I never wanted to pet your pet, meet your pet,
or greet your pet, only to beat your pet
That's why I was armed and dangerous
I never trusted dogs and I trusted dog owners
even less, for they were quick to say:
"He doesn't bite."
That's why I was armed and dangerous
My philosophy was, "If attacked then counterattack."
that's why I was armed and dangerous
Fortunately, only a few dogs got to taste
my wrath
I retired from the Postal Service in 2006 after 30 years
and so, I am no longer
Armed or dangerous

GOOD HELP

My girlfriend was my helper in my home-
improvement business
She was good, very good
Didn't do a lot of the work herself
but she was a good helper, very good
could anticipate my every need
Unlike the doctor in surgery, if I needed a certain tool
before asking or even looking for it, she was handing it to me
When I had to move to another spot to work
like a good neighbor, she was there
with the ladder and whatever else I needed
Her ability to anticipate what I needed
was uncanny since I didn't always know myself

DINNER MUSIC

Running home after a day of playing
in the woods,
I remember bursting into the kitchen
while mother was preparing dinner.
She always wore a white apron over what
she called one of her everyday dresses.
Because she was just starting dinner,
the aromas were just starting to permeate the air.
Like my dad, I headed straight to the stove,
removing tops from pots to see what was cooking.
And just as with my dad, mothers would
always say, "Get out of there.
You just came in from outside, go wash your
dirty hands and face."
After washing up, I went right back to looking
in the pots.
What truly made the day is when I asked
mother if we could have a pie for dessert.
After pondering a few moments, she said to my delight,
"Go pick me some apples…but you have
to peel them too. It was music to my ears.

HOW MOTHER MADE BISCUITS

Back in the 1940's and 50's, as much
as I loved Mother's hot biscuits
right from the oven; I loved watching
her make the biscuits.
Mother was an old fashioned country girl
and she made biscuits the old fashioned way—
with her hands.
In one kitchen cupboard there was a
metal bin where flour was stored.
The bottom of the bin was tapered like a funnel.
Fixed to the very bottom was a sifter
with a handle that could be turned to sift
some flour into a cup or bowl.
After sifting 4 heaping cups full of that self rising
flour, the only kind she used, she then
dumped the 4 cups into her big wooden pastry bowl.
She would then sprinkle over the flour,
2 big spoons of Clabber Girl Baking Powder;
the only brand she would use.
Next, came a dab of salt and 2 dabs
of sugar.
All the while she would be stirring and
tossing these dry ingredients
into that bowl of flour. She would make
a hole or valley into which she would
drop a hunk of lard (poor people's shortening).

From the bottle, she would pour over the lard some
buttermilk; the only milk suitable for biscuit making.
How much buttermilk?
One coffee cup full.
Then, instead of using a fork or spoon,
Mother would plunge her hand down into
that healthy gook of buttermilk and lard.
She would then mix and squeeze,
mix and squeeze, forcing that gook
to ooze between her fingers.
Gradually, she would bring in more flour
and as she did she would also mix
and squeeze, mix and squeeze.
Finally, she would withdraw her hand,
scraping off all of the mix still clinging
to her fingers and hand. This she folded
into that ball of dough.
She then felt the need…to knead.
The need to knead however, was only needed a little.
For biscuit dough unlike yeast dough,
need only a little kneading. Gentle and brief.
So gentle and so brief that the kneading needed
was done right in that big bowl.
Thus, there was no need for a dough scraper.
Did Mother then roll out the dough
onto a lightly floured surface with
a rolling pin?
Of course not!
Besides not owning a rolling pin,
Fannie Whitley didn't make biscuits that way.

She would pinch off a little piece of dough,
rolling it around in her hands like she was
making "patty cakes".
With the heel of her hand she would make
a small dent in each biscuit.
Because Mother preferred soft, fluffy biscuits,
she would place them touching one another in an
ungreased cake pan.
Mother's biscuits were always the same size except for
the last one; it was always a little bigger or a
little smaller than the rest.
When mother took her biscuits from the oven,
they were always the same—golden brown on the
top and bottom; light and fluffy in the middle.
You see, Mother made her biscuits the old
fashioned way—she made them good.

SITTING PRETTY

Ladies, if you are ever sitting on stage,
in a class play or on the front row
of your church, this is one of those times
that you will want to be "sitting pretty"
To sit pretty…please do something
with your knees
Keep your knees together one way or another
Cross your ankles, placing the left foot behind
and to the right of the right foot
Another thing that can be done,
slide both feet to the side, either one
Remember, the speaker would likely never care
to see your pretty underwear
And if you follow this little ditty
It will help you to keep sitting pretty

I GOT HER HAMMER

Mother spent her last years
living in a senior citizen's building
Most of the residents there knew her
and she was well liked
When mother passed away
she had very little to pass on
Besides her furniture, I got
two other things, a huge claw hammer
and a machete
Billy took the Louisville Slugger

GET OUT OF MY GARDEN!

As always dad was sitting at the head
of the dinner table which faced the window
All of a sudden like a kangaroo
he leapt from the table and flew upstairs
In an instant, we heard the sound of
a gigantic BOOM!
Through the windows we saw feathers flying
as dad had unloaded both barrells
on those pigeons in his garden
They, needless to say, left off pecking
his freshly planted seeds

PORK AND RED MEAT

Personally, I have a very fastidious taste
I'm what they call picky
Don't like a lot of food piled on my plate
I find it to be unappetizing
I am the bland man
I savor nothing with added flavor
I regard it as a waste, for it
spoils the foods natural taste
I consider any food as lame
If it has a silly sounding name
Thus, I would never eat a rutabaga
Name reminds me of a car called a Studebaker
The back looked just like the front
Couldn't tell whether it was going or coming
The same holds true for squash
The name is just too harsh
I don't care for okra
But the name doesn't sound too bad
I don't care for lamb
But does that mean that lamb is unhealthy?
I don't care for lobster
But does that mean that lobster is unfit to eat?
Something else about me
I never try anything new
If I haven't already had it
Then I don't like it

I don't care for condiments
Neither mustard, relish nor ketchup
And please no sauces; no A1, A2, hot or chili
No tartar, Worcestershire, no mambo, tabasco
or Italiano
Yes, a lot of foods I don't care for
But then that's my business
Probably there are foods you don't care for
Now that's your business
And just as I have no business
Trying to make your business my business
So likewise, you have no business trying
to make my business your business
In other words, if you don't eat pork
or red meat, then guess what?
Who cares, that's your business!

EMMA'S POCKET BOOKS (HANDBAGS)

Some ladies seem to love hats
Some ladies seem to love shoes
Some ladies seem to love dresses
Emma loves pocket books, handbags
Emma loves large pocket books,
Small pocket books,
Medium size pocket books,
Any kind of pocket book
Emma has pocket books by the hundreds
At least ten pocket books for each outfit
Buys them three or four at a time
Emma has pocket books for all occasions
For all seasons and for all reasons
Says she feels naked without a pocket book

SECTION 2: PLACES

Places, like people, have a number of meanings. Places as mentioned in this section most often refer to other countries, cities and towns. Visiting and studying other places helps one to become more rounded.

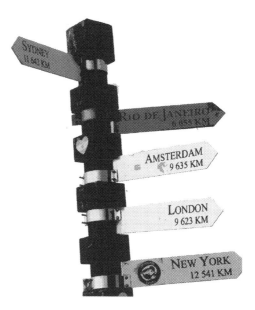

WORLD FAMOUS STREETS

It is the Kurfurstendamn
When it's Berlin that you're in
If it's Paris, the City of Light
Then you must say Champs Elysées
If it is in Rome where you now roam
Then the street to know is Via del Corso
For New York, New York
Whether night or day, its got to be Broadway

I AM A BERLINER

Strolling down the Kurfurstendamn
On one of my many visits to Berlin
I thought that if JFK could say it
Following only one visit then surely
I could say, "Ish bien ein Berliner."

A WEEK IN AMSTERDAM

With a bike rented for a day
And armed with a map of the city
I took on Amsterdam
Not that it was some kind of daunting
Challenge, for the city is laid out
Very well and the Dutch people are some
Of the nicest people that I have ever met
I was not even overwhelmed by the hundreds
Of bicyclists all around me as I stopped
Or took off from a traffic light
During the course of a week I visited
The Rijks museum and was able to see
Many of Rembrandt's paintings including
"The Night Watch"
Of course, there was the Vincent Van Gogh
Museum where I saw many of the works
Of that Dutch artist
I watched as machines with diamond
Tipped blades took hours to cut a diamond
Visited the Heineken Brewery and
Watched beer being brewed
Going from one attraction to another
I bought French Fries at one of Amsterdam's
Many French fry stands
The Anne Frank House and the story

Behind it proved very interesting
But something more interesting and fascinating
Was the many canals that dominate
The city

RED LIGHT DISTRICT

Passing by a shop window what
I thought was a scantily clad mannequin,
After further review, I discovered
It was a real live woman
Just as a store owner puts his merchandise
On display in his store window
In the Red Light District of Amsterdam
Prostitutes were on display in the
Windows of brothels

EUROPE ON $5.00 A DAY

When I was first there the book was out
Europe on five dollars a day
And it was true, in the 1960's
One could tour Europe on five
Dollars a day
In Amsterdam I stayed at a quaint
Bed and Breakfast for around two dollars
A night
Rented a bike for less than a dollar a day
Which left me with plenty enough
Money for lunch and dinner

HOME

Home is the place where one lives,

Be it a house, hut, tent or cave

It is the physical structure, the dwelling

Place with family or social unit or alone

It is a place considered to be a refuge

Or place of origin

So while people may wander

While people may roam

The place that many yearn to come back to

Is the place they call home

JUST SOMETHING TO DO

It was not that we appreciated culture
It was just something to do
We were poor living in Washington, DC
And so places that were free
We took advantage of
Every Sunday we went to one
Of the Smithsonian Museums
"Studied" art at the National Gallery
Talked to congressmen inside the
U.S. Capitol Building
Walked up the steps of the Supreme Court
True, we didn't fully appreciate these
Historical treasures
Touring them, for us, was just something
To do

SNOWBALL FIGHT IN PARIS

I was in the U.S. Airforce in 1963
Stationed in Sembach Germany,
Three of my buddies and I
Decided to take a trip to Paris
Sgt. Homsby assured us that
His old Pontiac was up to the trip
Found out later that he had lied
Normal driving time from where
We were was something like two hours
It took us eighteen, we had snow
Plus, the car broke down three times
Two things from that trip stand out
In my mind
Looking at the city from the
Eiffel Tower
And getting in a snowball fight
With strangers as we walked down
The Champs Elysées

SECTION 3: THINGS

If it is not a person or place
Then it is most assuredly a thing. Hence,
One definition of thing is an inanimate object:
Her enthusiasms are more for things than for
People. Also, when the exact name for something
Has been forgotten or is not known then it
Becomes a thingamabob or thingamajig.

RETIREMENT-NOTHING TO DO

To see how retirement would be
John first took 30 days leave
After one week John was through
Came back saying he was bored, nothing to do
I have heard others complain saying it too
That they couldn't handle retirement, nothing to do
Nothing to do, nothing to do!
Living in metropolitan Washington, DC
Nothing to do, nothing to do
Don't say there's nothing to do
Rather, say you're scared to do anything
but go to work
Because there is plenty to do
More than enough to do
I doubt anyone would be bored by volunteering
To work at a soup kitchen for a few days
It could be a hospital or a homeless shelter
And when not doing that, what about all
Of the free things, the many monuments
Museums, art galleries, libraries, parks and
The national zoo
There are many free classes taught on
Almost every subject you could imagine
Wanna pick up on the latest dance step?
Sharpen your golf game?
Learn how to do your own taxes?

43

Learn how to play tennis?
Learn how to play the greatest card
Game ever, pinochle
It just so happens that I
teach pinochle 101
Want to learn? Give me a call
Now if you should retire
and you have a little money
answer these questions:
How many times have you been
to Sierra Leon, Johanesburg,
Paris, London, Rome or Alaska?
I am a retiree, have I been bored?
Not for a minute,
TOO MUCH TO DO!

I AM A FLOWER

I am a flower
People prize me for my beautiful shapes
and colors and for my delightful
fragrances
Because of my beauty I am a favorite
form of decoration
People sometimes use me to express their
deepest feelings
I am often placed on graves
I am used at weddings to symbolize love,
faithfulness and long life
Some of us have a religious significance
I am a flower, tell me please,
How may I serve you?

TREES

I am sure there will never be
Another plant quite like a tree.
My feelings about trees I guess
It is because they are so statuesque
Some trees grow so high
That they literally touch the sky.
Others grow so wide
That through their trunk a car you could drive.
Some trees grow so old
That their true age cannot be told.
Trees are never ever all alone
For a host of critters call a tree their home.
Trees also give us many helpful goods.
Most useful are the many kinds of woods.
Trees supply many other useful products;
an unending array of luscious fruits and nuts.
Some trees are especially good friends.
For some produce substances used as medicines.
Trees are some amazing things.
Somewhat like human beings.
Thus, I believe there will never be
another plant quite like a tree.

THE WHIRLYBIRD

The whirlybird can do almost all of the tricks of the
legendary flying carpet
It can go straight up or straight down
It can fly forward, backwards or even sideways
It can also stay in one spot in the air and then turn
completely around, hover
Humans have devised numerous ways of using
these birds; on the farm, in industry, in public service
as well as in the military
There is no bird like the whirlybird or as it is
commonly called, the helicopter

IT'S CALLED A LEVEL

A level is one of a builder's
most essential tools.
With it he can check to see if
a horizontal surface is straight or
whether a vertical surface is plumb.
Houses sometimes have walls that
are not straight because the ground
has caused them to shift.
Sometimes the walls are not straight
because the builder abandoned his level.
A builder without a level is like
a doctor without a stethoscope
Like a firefighter without water

MY FAVORITE THINGS

Hammers

Nails

Drills

Screwdrivers

Screws

Lumber

Saws

Sheetrock

Joint compound

Tape measures

Squares

Levels

Faucets that leak

Floors that squeak

These are a few of my favorite things

For I am a handyman

WINDOWS

WindoWindoW
I   I
N   N
D   D
O   O
WindoWindoW

WindoWindoW   The more windows the
I   I   more   light
N   N   and   the
D   D   more   air
O   O   will come into the house
WindoWindoW

An opening in a   The converse is also
wall. An opening   true   fewer
put there not for   windows will mean
access but to let   Less air and less light
in light and air.

A DOOR

A door is any movable barrier in a wall used to close off access to a room, a building, a vehicle or a covered enclosure, typically consisting of a panel made of wood, glass or metal that swings on hinges. Also, the  entrance way to a room, building or passage as in: Go through that door and then turn left or it can be a way by which something is gained as education may be said to be a door to success

A BACKHOE

Just so there is no misunderstanding
A backhoe is a machine
A power driven excavating machine
An earth mover

It somewhat resembles a mechanical monster
With its hinged bucket at the end
Of a long jointed arm

Two stabilizer legs enable it to stand up off of the
ground so the wheels won't roll when it digs

A backhoe digs by drawing its bucket
Toward the machine and scooping up dirt

Often at the other end of a backhoe is found a front
loader

When the operator wishes to use this feature,
he merely turns his swivel seat around where he finds
another set of levers and pedals

The front loader scoops up dirt by pushing its bucket
forward toward a pile or mound of dirt

The front bucket also helps to stabilize it when it
stands up

About the size of a small truck some backhoes have
four wheels and all of the safety features necessary
for it to be driven on the street

There are a number of attachments that can be
affixed to a backhoe enabling it to do a variety of
jobs

It can be fitted with a large jackhammer for breaking
up concrete roads

It can be equipped with a tamper to tamp down fill
dirt

A big sawblade for grinding down tree stumps
With an auger for drilling post holes
Two forks and it becomes a forklift

It can also serve as a small crane lifting objects too
heavy for the workmen

Like its airborne friend, the helicopter
The backhoe is one versatile machine

DOORBELLS, INTERCOMS, CAMERAS

It used to be that a doorbell told you
that someone was at your door

It used to be that an intercom
allowed you to talk to whoever
was at your door

Add a small camera and you now see who's at the door

But with a smart phone
you can do all of the above
and not even be at home

THE FIRST CELL PHONES

Do you remember the first cell phones?
When they could not fit in your pocket?

When they resembled an attache case
When they had a two foot antenna
and a big battery pack for power

If you were around in the mid 1980's
then you just may remember
the first cell phones

THE HORSE, OF COURSE!

For humans it was one of the most useful
animals for thousands of years
It was, the horse, of course!
What once provided humans with the fastest
and surest way to travel on land
It was, the horse, of course!
Hunters were able to chase and shoot
animals for food while riding them
It was, the horse, of course!
Soldiers once charged into battle mounted
on them
It was, the horse, of course!
The pioneers and cowboys who settled
the American west would likely have called them
"Man's best friend"
It was, the horse, of course!
What animals still thrill crowds at races, rodeos
circuses, carnivals, parades, and shows?
It is, the horse, of course!
Adults and children today take riding lessons,
join riding clubs, because of something they are still
fascinated with
It is, the horse, of course!

SECTION 4: CELESTIAL AND ATMOSPHERIC PHENOMENA

Celestial pertains to the sky or heavens,
to the divine. Atmospheric pertains to that
which surrounds any star or planet.

THE SUN

Like a gigantic light bulb
it lights up the earth
Like a humongous blast furnace
it heats up our planet
The sun is a gift from the
Father of celestial lights
The giver of every good gift and
every perfect present
He makes the sun shine upon all alike,
the wicked and the good
The sun, we should be very thankful for
Life on earth would be no fun
without the sun
For without the sun, life on earth,
there would be none

HAILSTORMS

Windstorms,
    Rainstorms,
      Hailstorms
Of these three atmospheric disturbances,
try never to get caught in a hailstorm.
You see, these lumps of ice called hail
can range from the size of peas
to the size of oranges or larger
Hailstones fall to the ground at a speed of
about 22 miles per hour
Thus, hail as you might imagine
can do some serious damage.
Hail can break windows, damage roofs,
as well as dent cars and airplanes.
Crop damage caused by hail is in the
hundreds of millions of dollars every year.
Occasionally, people caught in the open
in severe hailstorms have been killed
So having raindrops falling on my head
is something I might not dread
But hailstones? Hail no!

IT'S A METEOR!

Look! Up in the sky
It's a shooting star
No, it's a meteor

What is a meteor?
A meteor is a bright streak of light
seen briefly in the sky
Meteors result when chunks of metal
or rocks called meteoroids enter
the Earth's atmosphere from space
Air friction makes the meteoroid so hot
that it glows and creates a trail
of hot glowing gases
This makes them look like falling stars

DEW

From whence comes the dew?
Those tiny drops of water that are found
Coming not only from the night air
But also from the ground

It also comes from a different source
From plants and other vegetation
When moisture evaporates into the air
Dew is the result of this condensation

FROST, WHEN DOES IT COME?

What is frost? And when does it come?
Frost is a pattern of ice crystals formed
From water vapor on grass, window panes,
And other exposed surfaces near the ground.
Frost occurs mainly when it is cold and cloudless,
When the air temperature drops below freezing.
Frost, like it's cousin dew, is also a freak, and
Everybody knows that "freaks come out at night."

TORNADOES

I am a rotating funnel cloud that sometimes sweeps
down upon the earth

A powerful, twisting windstorm I am
My winds are more violent than any other storm that
occurs on earth

They whirl around the center of the storm at speeds
of more than 200 miles per hour

My winds whirl counterclockwise in the
Northern hemisphere but clockwise in the
Southern hemisphere

Generally, I don't last very long,
often less than an hour

While I whirl throughout the world
My favorite place to play is the good ole U.S. of A

STARS DON'T REALLY TWINKLE

Twinkle, twinkle little star is not
Scientifically true
For stars don't really twinkle
They only appear to

They appear to twinkle
When we look up there
And that is only because
We see them through layers of air

Not only do stars not twinkle
But calling them little, we cannot say
Stars only look little because of
Being so far away

Also, wishing upon a star
Is something done in vain
Stars don't grant wishes
It is only beauty they have as gain

EARTHQUAKES (ALL SHOOK UP)

An earthquake is a sudden shaking
or shock in the earth
You might say that when a certain area
of the earth gets "all shook up";
and if you experience an earthquake
of sufficient magnitude, then you
very well may get "All Shook Up"

TSUNAMI

When you look at me,
imagine that you don't see the "T"
This is because the "T" in my name
is silent, therefore I am pronounced as (t)sōō nä mē

What am I? I am a huge sea wave
caused by a submarine disturbance,
such as an earthquake or volcanic eruption;
also popularly, but incorrectly
called a tidal wave

HURRICANES

In the western Pacific Ocean I am called a typhoon

In the Indian Ocean they call me a cyclone

But in the North Atlantic and the North Pacific,
hurricane is my name

By either name, what I am is a storm measuring
200 to 300 miles in diameter

The winds in my center around my eye blow at
speeds of 75 miles per hour or more

What is my eye? Believe it or not my eye is a calm
area of about 20 miles in my center

It used to be that we were named only after females
While humans give us nice personal names
The measure of our destruction is what gives us fame

I LOVE NASTY WEATHER

Unlike most people, I hate warm sunshiny days —
the so-called nice weather

I love the so-called nasty weather
Yes, I prefer the days that are rainy, cold, damp,
misty or snowy

When asked why, I always explain that such weather
tends to keep people in their houses and so,
I could deliver the mail in peace

WALKING THE DOG

The rain came down, not in a heavy downpour
But rather, in a steady light drizzle
as if from a sprinkler system
The man walking his dog had no hat, no umbrella
nor any rain gear
However, his little dog was outfitted with the cutest
little raincoat and rain hat that you ever did see

LIGHTNING-WRONG TIME, WRONG PLACE?

Sometimes calamity befalls us simply for being in
the wrong place at the wrong time
Thus, when Buddy Boy was standing on that
manhole cover and it was struck by
lightning, it could be said that he was
at the wrong place at the wrong time
Thankfully, he was only knocked out,
not knocked dead!

PREDICTING THE WEATHER

Predicting the weather is a science but
it is not an exact science
The forecast of meteorologists are therefore
sometimes off, occasionally wrong
This is because there are so many possible
weather conditions and these conditions
change so quickly

SPRINGTIME

Many have been the songs and poems
written about springtime
For there is no time like springtime
The number of daylight hours increases
The temperatures get warrmer
Creation awakens in spring
Snow melts, flowers blossom,
hibernating animals come out
For humans the spring thing
Is to have a spring fling
So we have festivals

SMOKE IS

Smoke is that non-salubrious vapor
made up of small particles of
carbonaceous matter

Smoke has but a few helpful uses
including curing meat and
protecting orchards

Smoke is the reason why chimneys exist
Smoke is the biggest cause of death in
house fires
Smoke is something no sane person ever
wants in his or her nostrils

SECTION 5: LOVE AND MARRIAGE

It was once said that love and marriage go together
like a horse and carriage. Sad to say however, that
just as the horse and carriage is no longer a common
mode of transportation, neither is love and marriage
an enduring association.

THINK LIKE A MAN, BUT ACT LIKE A LADY

In male/female relationships
Women, ladies are encouraged
To think like a man
But to act like ladies
Is this good advice?
Is this something that can be accomplished
Yes, can a lady think like a man
But then act like a lady
The problem with this is that most men don't think
At least not with their head
Not even with their heart
But with other things instead
Many men think with their stomachs
Most though, think with something else
What most men think with
Is found below the belt

A MONSTER IN MY DREAMS

After my wife and I have had
one of our serious heart to heart talks,
a cigarette is never what I wanted
Being adherents of the Scriptures,
smoking is something we could not do
After we will have talked it out,
cleared the air, what I usually wanted
and what I would usually do is go
to sleep
And when I would go to sleep,
a certain nocturnal vision
I would always have
And in this vision,
I would always be running
Running like Gump
Running because almost always
there was a monster in my dreams
A huge hideous dragon-like monster
with long sharp teeth
Always after me, always seeking
to devour me
And just like in the cartoons,
always just one bite behind my behind
Yes, whenever we had one of those talks
that really cleared the air

As when we were in complete agreement,
that's when I would go to sleep
And that's when there would be
A monster in my dreams

SOMETHING BEAUTIFUL

What could be more beautiful than the growth of a plant
Not just any plant but a plant that you were given
because it was considered as good as dead.
A plant whose vital signs were almost impossible to find
A plant drooped over as if it were carrying
the weight of a mountain

A plant whose smile had turned upside-down into a frown
but you took the structure and nursed it back to life
Its soil you changed and rearranged, and with the best plant
food that money could buy, you fed it
Only purified water you gave it to drink

You talked to it, encouraged it, built it up,
told it how beautiful it was becoming
and how pleased you were with its progress
Your work with it was imbued with
the spirit of determination
Finally, one day you found it standing statuesque,
in all of its radiant glory
In the splendor of a plant, the leaves of which waxed poetic
about the magnificent job you had done.

You could hardly wait to see the giver of that plant
To tell them, to show them what had
become of the plant you had received DOA
What could be more beautiful than this story?

A LOVE AFFAIR INVOLVING TWO PEOPLE

What could be more beautiful than a love affair
A love affair between a man and a woman
A love affair thought to have been over
But was rekindled and nurtured
So that it resurged, bloomed and blossomed
So that it led them to Holy Matrimony

YOU HAD BETTER STOP ABUSING HER

Men, if you learn nothing else
here's a bit of advice you should keep
Never abuse and misuse your lady
then get drunk or go to sleep

And here's a very good reason,
because it might just be for you
that when it comes the time
your waking up may be very hard to do

NO DATING

In Bible times, it did not exist.
there was no such thing as dating.
When it came time to marry
it was the parents who were the matchmakers

Now, before you begin to criticize
there is something you must realize
That God's people had no problem with this
as it was fine and acceptable in God's eyes

What about God's people today?
Dating is a way to find a marriage mate
because it's not a game, not recreation
If not looking to marry then they don't date

What's wrong with dating for fun,
dating for recreation?
It's what dating most often leads to;
that sin called fornication.

IF IT SUITS THEM, FINE

In some cultures even today
couples don't spend time alone
If they are to get together
they must have a chaperon

In permissive western societies
where almost anything goes
By the third date, max
they're already out of their clothes

And any culture or society
that doesn't view dating this way

They laugh at and ridicule
about them having nothing good to say

WHY DOES THE FIREFLY FLASH?

(Or Why Does the Lightning Bug Light?)

On many early summer nights
fireflies literally fill the air
Flashing their lights in the night,
they appear to be everywhere

Why does the firefly flash?
He is signaling to potential mates
For as he flashes, he also looks
The right flash from a female he awaits

When he gets the right flash from a female
he lights out after her, making a mad dash
Determined to light up that female
who gave him that flash

SECTION 6: NATURAL RESOURCES

Natural resources are those
products and features from
the earth that permit it to
support life and satisfy people's needs.
Hence, land and water are natural resources.
This includes the biological resources
on the land and in the water.
Rivers are some of the greatest
natural resources.
They have been important to
transportation and trade for centuries.
For explorers, traders and pioneers in
North and South American rivers
were their main travel route
with settlements being built along them.
A good example, St. Paul, St. Louis,
Memphis, and New Orleans are
all built along the Mississippi River.

COAL

Coal, like gold is mined from the earth
But that's where the similarity ends
Gold is an attractive precious metal
While coal is an ugly dirty rock
Coal, however, is a vital energy source
Coal can be ignited and burned to
produce energy in the form of heat
One of the many uses of the energy
from coal is the production of electricity
One of the main sources of energy in all
industrial countries, coal is being
replaced by petroleum and natural gas

OIL

So useful, so beneficial, so valuable
So some people refer to it as black gold
It is, of course, oil (petroleum)
That black goo that comes up from the ground
And when refined provides a laundry list of products,
chief of which is gasoline

Oil has become an international bargaining chip
Oil exporting countries have been able to use oil as a
weapon against those nations that don't produce
enough oil for themselves or that try to live above
their energy means

GOING GREEN

Going green
What does that mean?
It means going back to our roots
And our roots are in the earth
Because we were created from the earth
To live on the earth
And so we must respect the earth
After years of disrespecting the earth
We are now encouraged to go green
To show some respect
Is it too late? Could be
But even if it is
It is still the right thing to do

WHEN IS ICE NOT SO NICE?

When is ice not so nice?
Ice, which is frozen water, is not
always very nice
Ice is nice in a glass with one's
favorite beverage poured over it
Ice is nice as a refrigerant to preserve
and keep food cold
Ice is nice in air conditioning systems
to keep us cool in summer
Ice is not so nice when it covers
the streets and sidewalks
When it comes in the form of snow,
sleet, frost and hail
When it causes car crashes,
as well as, slips, trips and falls.
That is when ice is not so nice

IRON AND STEEL

Iron can refer to both an element and to a metal
Like coal, we get iron ore by two basic methods,
From open pit mining and underground mining
And just as gasoline is refined oil,
So likewise steel is refined iron
Steel is iron cooked well-done
With a few other metals thrown in
Cooking temperature, about 3,000 degrees

COPPER

With my alloys
I have been made into
Such things as
water pipes
electrical wiring
doors knobs
drawer pulls
candle holders
Also
mail boxes
light fixtures
and locks

FROM WHENCE CAME THE
WORD VOLCANO?

From whence came the word volcano?
It was from the ancient Romans
that this word was first heard
The word volcano comes from Vulcan
the name the Romans gave to their god of fire
Vulcan, they believed, lived beneath a
volcanic island off the Italian coast
And so they called the island Volcano

A volcano is actually an opening
or hole in the earth's surface through
which fire, lava, and hot gases erupt

Volcanic eruptions we have always found
To be both awe inspiring and terrifying

LAVA

Deep in the middle of the
earth it is hot; very, very hot
So hot that even rocks melt
Inside the earth this molten rock is
called magma
When it erupts from a volcano
it is then called lava
Highly fluid lava hardens into folded
sheets of rock called pahoehoe
The stickier lava cools into rough, jagged
sheets of rock called by a word
that would make you think you were
being examined by a doctor

The word is pronounced ah ah
But spelled aa

SECTION 7: RELIGION

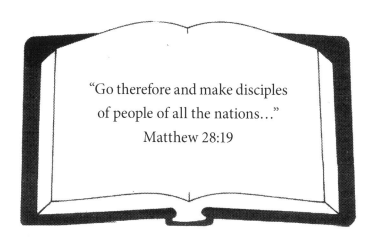

"Go therefore and make disciples
of people of all the nations…"
Matthew 28:19

"I don't discuss religion" you'll sometimes hear people say
"I don't believe in organized religion" you'll also sometimes hear.
This is usually because religion is highly personal and highly
controversial. Jesus Christ, the founder of Christianity didn't
subscribe to either notion. Jesus trained his disciples, then
sent them out by two's to proclaim his message.
His parting instructions to them were
"Go, therefore and make disciples of people of all the nations,
baptizing them in the name of the
Father and of the Son and of the holy spirit teaching them
to observe all the things I have commanded you.
And look I am with you all of the days."
This means that those professing to be Christians
have an obligation to proselytize.

ALMIGHTY GOD IS SELF SUFFICIENT

Almight God is self sufficient
    This means that God needs
    absolutely nothing and
    absolutely nobody
This means that God
    never gets lonely,
    tired or bored
This means that
    while God has
    trillions of angels
    in heaven, he
    needs them not
This means that while God has
    billions of humans on earth,
    he needs them not
This means that when a
    human dies it is not
    God calling them home
    for earth is the home of
    humans

                       Psa. 115:6

RELIGION

Some folks have an aversion to religion
Some regard religion as a poison
Some blame religion as the cause for
most of the world's problems
Some believe religion to be one of our
greatest assets
Some avoid discussing religion,
regarding it as too personal and too controversial
Jesus Christ, the founder of Christianity,
openly and eagerly discussed religion
Jesus Christ traveled the land of Palestine
discussing his religion
Jesus Christ trained his disciples and
sent them out by two's to proclaim God's word
Jesus Christ's final instructions to his
disciples was for them to take his
message to the whole world

THE HOLY SCRIPTURES

Those men used by God to write
the holy book, never refered to it
As the Holy Bible
They always called their holy writings
Holy writings or holy scriptures
Never used the words Old or New Testament
Never called Gospel writers Saint Matthew,
Saint Mark, Saint Luke, or Saint John
The word Bible is not from the holy scriptures
but from the Latin by way of the Greeks

KEYS TO THE KINGDOM

Keys to the kingdom of the heavens
were given to Peter
But what were those keys?
They certainly were not implements
designed to open a literal lock
Key can also refer to new and vital knowledge,
information, or to crucial facts
So Peter dispensed knowledge and information
enabling his country men to get in line to
gain access to the kingdom
Thus, Peter used the keys while
he was on earth, not in heaven
There is only one access controller to heaven
and that is Almighty God
Jesus himself admitted that not even
he had the power or authority to grant
access to heaven

WHEN WAS SATAN KICKED OUT?

When was Satan kicked out of heaven?
> It was not in the time of Adam and Eve

When was Satan kicked out of heaven?
> It was not in the days of Job

When was Satan kicked out of heaven?
> It was not in the days of Jesus Christ

When was Satan kicked out of heaven?
> It was only mentioned in the Revelation

When was Satan kicked out of heaven?
> It was in the last days not long ago

DO YOU APPRECIATE YOUR GIFT?

Once we give something to another person
it is theirs to do with as they wish
When they put the gift to good use
we call that appreciation
When they misuse and/or abuse the gift
we call that a lack of appreciation
We have all been given a gift from our Creator,
the gift of life
When Almighty God looks at how we are using
our gift will he see appreciation?
Yes, will He have cause for jubilation?

FAME AND GLORY

For himself he wants fame and glory
He wants it to be that everybody knows his name
He wants his name to stand out
To rise above all others
He wants no one to question who he is
He wants all to know who he is
When names are brought up
He wants his name right up there
When name dropping is done
He wants his to be the one
He wants his enemies to shutter
At the very sound of his name
He wants his name to evoke awe and respect
Yes, for himself he wants fame and glory
And what's wrong with wanting fame and glory
For yourself when you deserve it
When you are God

ORGANIZED RELIGION

When people say they are against
organized religion
What they generally mean is that
they are against the traditional,
long established churches.
To be against organized religion
is to be against God himself
For if religion is not organized,
then it is disorganized or unorganized
and therefore unacceptable to God
who the Bible says is a "God of Order,"
not disorder.

FUNERALS

It was not meant that we
should ever attend funerals
And here's the reason why
We were created to live forever
It was not His purpose that we
Should ever die

DO YOU BELIEVE IN GOD?

It is not uncommon today to hear a person
say that they don't believe in
God. But guess what?
Whether or not
one
believes in God is a moot question. For God
exists whether one knows it or not
or believes it or not. Disbelief
is inconsequential and
since God believes
in only those who
are earnestly
seeking him
then the
all
important question is not do you
believe in God but rather,
does God believe in
You?

FIGHTING COVID-19

If the love for your neighbor
    is really true
Then during this pandemic,
    this you should always do

Regularly wash your hands
"Social distance," leave some space
Always wear some kind of mask Yes,
hide that pretty face

If you are a senior
You should especially beware
If you have respiratory problems
Then take the utmost care

Stay yourself at home Just
as much as you can Go out
only for essentials
Go out only when planned

A REAL CHRISTIAN IS A
DIFFERENT KIND OF PERSON

A real Christian is not like a lot of other people

A real Christian is a different kind of person

A real Christian is a real good imitator of Jesus Christ
A real Christian is one of good moral character
A real Christian therefore is loving and kind

A real Christian is a real student of the Scriptures
A real Christian is meek and mild
A real Christian is warm and friendly
A real Christian is bold and strong
A real Christian is a real busy spreader
Of the Word of God

BIBLICAL MOVIES

Who needs a movie
To bolster their faith
Not real Christians
Just those who perpetrate
Biblical movies by worldlings
are bound to be flawed
Therefore, real Christians
are not by them awed
Real Christians know the truth,
They've got it right
They therefore walk by faith
and not by sight

EVERLASTING LIFE...ON EARTH

In the Garden of Eden there were many trees
How do we know? The Bible tell us so, Gen. 2:9

In the Garden there were two trees with given names
How do we know? The Bible tells us so, Gen. 2:9

They were the tree of life and the tree of the
knowledge of good and evil
How do we know? The Bible tells us so, Gen. 2:9

Eating from the tree of the knowledge of good and evil
was a capital offense, death
How do we know? The Bible tells us so, Gen. 2:17

Eating from the tree of life meant everlasting life on earth for the eater
How do we know? The Bible tells us so, Gen. 3:22

To carry out the death sentence God put Adam and Eve out
How do we know? The Bible tells us so, Gen. 3:24

To block the way to the tree of life God stationed angels
How do we know? The Bible tells us so, Gen. 3:24

It was God's purpose that humans live forever in paradise
on earth, and His purpose never fails
How do we know? The Bible tells us so, Gen 1:28; Isa. 55:11

Jesus verified that paradise on earth would be restored
when he told the evil doer executed alongside of him
"Truly I say this to you today
That you will be with me in Paradise"

Jesus was not saying that the evil doer
executed with him would on that day
be with him in heaven since Jesus
did not go to heaven on that day

IN GOD'S IMAGE

Created in God's image
What does that mean?
Not that we look like God For
God is a spirit
It means that humans have
certain qualities like God
Certain qualities that animals don't have
Only humans have true wisdom
Which starts with knowing
God Only humans have true love
Based on an unselfish interest in another
Only humans manifest true justice
The ability to calcuate fairness and impartiality
Only humans have true power
the ability to harnest the elements for mans good
Never, ever will you hear an animal say
about any of these things; "Oh, I can do that."

FINAL PART OF THE DAYS, TIME OF THE END (MATTHEW 24)

War and reports of war
More war now than ever before
Scriptures says this would happen, when?
Final part of the days, time of the end

Crime and violence everywhere
People acting like they just don't care
Scripture says this would happen, when?
Final part of the days, time of the end

Earthquakes, food shortages, one place after another
More at this time than any other
Scripture says this would happen, when?
Final part of the days, time of the end

Disease and pestilence taking their toll
Wiping out some young but mostly old
Scriptures says this world happen, when?
Final part of the days, time of the end

Many false prophets would arise
Misleading many with all their lies
Scriptures says this would happen, when?
Final part of the days, time of the end

True disciples hated and betrayed
But never ever to be dismayed
Scripture says this would happen, when?
Final part of the days, time of the end

To have one's salvation be made sure
Each and every would have to endure
Scriptures says this would happen, when?
Final part of the days, time of the end

Kingdom good news would have to be preached
People the world over would have to be reached
Scriptures says this would happen, when?
Final part of the days, time of the end

INEXCUSABLE

To not believe in his existence
God says is inexcusable
Why? Because all of the
Things around us, the
earth, sun, moon
and stars
all testify
To
His existence. Just as it
is written: "Every house
was constructed by
Someone but He
who constructed
all things
is God

HIS PURPOSE HAS NOT CHANGED

God told Adam and Eve to have children
And fill the earth with them.
He also told them to replenish the earth
And subdue it
And what did that mean but to cultivate
the earth extending the paradise earthwide.
Thus, it was God's purpose that humans live
forever on a paradise earth.

THE WORD

Before coming to Earth
In case you never heard
The one we know as Jesus Christ
In heaven was called the
Word God's only direct creation
The Word was the only one
For this reason he is also called
God's only begotten Son

John 1:14 KJV

WHAT IS COVID-19?

COVID-19 is an infectious flu-like disease
Caused by the coronovirus
COVID-19 is a pandemic killing people
By the hundreds of thousands
COVID-19 like the flu, is a respiratory disease
That is inhaled
COVID-19 caused the shutdown of businesses
And commerce of whole nations
COVID-19 closed schools and sports arenas,
Professional and amateur
COVID-19 brought us quarantine, p-p-e,
And "social distancing"
COVID-19, discoverd in 2019, is pestilence
and pestilence is part of the sign of the last days,
The time of the end

OLD AGE AND DEATH

Old age and death
Two of the most dreadful things
Two of the very, very worst
Ever to come upon human beings

Was this God's purpose?
That we get sick, grow old and die
The answer is an unequivocal no!
And here's the reason why

In the Garden God planted "the tree of life"
Eating from it meant death, never, no never
Eating from it enabled one to live
endlessly, eternally, forever and ever

Gen. 2:9 KJV

WHAT MEANS JOHN 3:16?

You see it on bumper stickers on cars
You see it on banners in sports stadiums
and arenas
You see it on every kind of commodity
made by human hands
Other than the 23rd Psalm, it is probably
one of the most popular Bible verses
there is
This gives rise to the question:
"What means John 3:16?
It means that because of His great love
for mankind, God provided
the ransom of His only begotten Son
With those exercising strong faith in him
gaining everlasting life, but destruction
for all others.

DID GOD CALL THEM HOME?

At Aunt Sally's funeral, I listened very carefully
to the preacher, very carefully as he uttered
those troubling words.
He said that God had called Aunt Sally home,
that he needed another angel.
Those words "God called her home" cut through
me like a sharp knife.
Did that mean that God sent the burgular
who broke into her house and beat her to death?
At Uncle Jake's funeral, it was said that
God had called him home.
Did this mean that God sent that drunk driver
to crash into his car?
When 8-year-old Chelsey was killed by a stray bullet
the preacher said that God had called
her to be one of his angels.
Does this mean that God sent
that drug dealer who accidently shot her
when he was trying to shoot someone else?
At the funeral of the drug addict super star singer
who died from an overdose of drugs
it was said that God wanted that
beautiful voice in heaven.
Does this mean that God encourages
drug abuse?
Is God responsible for all of the deaths

and murders that take place?
When people die is God calling them home?
How could he since they never lived in
heaven with God?
And how could he since none of the
aforementioned were said to have been
"born again" Christians, a prerequisite
for going to heaven.

WHEN SHOULD MURDERERS BE FORGIVEN?

It is said that capital punishment denies
the possibiliy of redemption and rehabilitation.
This is oh so very true
But then that's what capital punishment is supposed to do

The basis for forgiveness is that an offender must
truly be sorry and must rectify the wrong
If he has taken money, he must pay it back
If he has taken a life, he must pay that back

So as soon as the murderer expresses remorse
and brings his victim back to life
Then he will have been redeemed,
Then he will have been rehabilitated.

Then he should be forgiven.

MURDERERS: USELESS PEOPLE

Of all the people on this earth,
Who are the ones who have no worth?
Who should not be allowed to live?
Who to society have nothing at all to give?
Who have committed such a heinous deed?
Who is it that execution is what they need?
Who but the murderer fits this bill?
Who but the murderer is it right to kill?

AFTER LIFE

After life what is there?
After life is simple
After life there is death
And what is death
Death is simple
Death is the opposite of life
Death is the state of unconsciousness
Death is when your love, hate and
    jealousy have all ended,
when you know nothing, see nothing
    and feel nothing
Death is when you are alive only
    in someone else's memory

NOT BY SIGHT

He no longer favors a particular land
So no land is holy anymore
He no longer favors an earthly city
So no city is holy anymore
He no longer favors earthly buildings
So no earthly buildings are holy anymore
He no longer favors a single race or nation
So no race or nation is holy anymore
His people now come from all races and nations
They are an international brotherhood
His people don't need visible objects for worship
They worship with spirit and truth
His people don't trek to any particular place
They know that it is not where but how one worships
His people don't worship relics, any kind of shrines, buildings, or lands
They walk by faith and not by sight

A DIFFERENT KIND OF FIGHT

I will never again carry a gun
I will never again seek to take another's life
I will never again support any nation's military
None of these things will I ever do again
because I am now on another mission
I have enlisted in Christ's army
I engage in no carnal warfare
We engage in spiritual warfare
Our weapon of choice is the sword
of the spirit, God's word, the Bible
We fight to overthrow strongly
entrenched things, like false teachings
and false reasonings
We fight to help others to gain the real life,
everlasting life, eternal life, endless life

SECTION 8: PHILOSOPHY

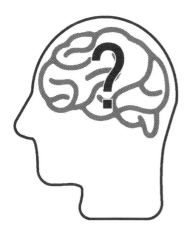

"Philosophy," is a word derived from Greek roots meaning love and pursuit of wisdom by intellectual means. The system of values by which one lives. Philosophy and philosophers can at times be strange bedfellows and so care has to be exercised when dealing with either one.

DWB

DWB can get you hurt
DWB can get you killed
So when stopped for DWB
Don't get upset, just chill

Cooperate with the authority
Don't give them any flak
Even when you suspect that
You were stopped for Driving While Black

If you feel that you just must make a fuss
Wait until you get away
Wait, wait until you get home
Wait to live another day

WHEN STOPPED BY THE POLICE

Whenever I am stopped by the police, I immediately get out my driver's license and registration card. I roll down the window and hand it to the officer as he walks up. I accord him or her the utmost respect. Always yes sir, yes ma'am, no sir, no ma'am. And guess what? They generally let me go

WHEN IS IT TIME TO HATE?

Since there is a time for everything
under the sun
A time to love and a time to hate
When is it the time to hate?
The time to hate is all of the time
This is because the time to hate
is determined by what we are to hate
So what is it that we are to hate
all of the time?
All of the time we are to hate
what is bad

Ps 97:10

PROBLEM OR SOLUTION

In an earlier generation the government
And all of those in power were referred to
As the "establishment" and the cry
From those who felt downtrodden
Was "down with the establishment."

Problem was they had no solution!
Down with the establishment but up
With what?

Likewise today, they are many who
Bemoan the system but like their
Predecessors they have no solution

Complain is all they can do
Perhaps they need to be reminded of the
Old adage, that you are a part
Of the problem unless you are a
Part of the solution.

THE THRILL OF THE KILL

Why are certain policemen still shooting
And killing unarmed black men?
Could it be how it makes them feel?
Fun with the gun, the thrill of the kill
Some find no joy in the participation in
Anything called a de-escalation
They want to have fun with their gun
And feel the thrill of the kill
Wasting those whom they regard as utter waste
Some folks will poo poo this explanation
Will condemn me for such an insinuation
Will not believe that some officers are having fun
When emptying and reloading their gun
They will not believe that some, like big
game hunters, get a thrill from the kill

DANGEROUS PHILOSOPHIES

Like racism and sexism
Both patriotism and nationalism
Can be dangerous philosophies

Dangerous because they both
Border on worship of one's nation,
A form of idolatry.

Dangerous because they are both
Emotional attitudes; attitudes
That sometimes become exaggerated
Or distorted.

Because of patriotism and nationalism
Some nations feel they have a moral
Responsibility to force their form
Of government and culture on what
They deem as "inferior nations"
Have you not seen this?

A CHANGED MAN

Though he wore the uniform of a soldier
a fighter, a killer
He was a kind man, like a good doctor
with a mild temper and even disposition
But then came the war in Iraq,
constant carnage
The horrors of that war took a toll on him
John came home from the war a changed man
Post traumatic stress syndrome
John was now a mean man
volatile and hostile
What a difference a war makes

TINTED WINDOWS

If driving while black is a hazard that everybody now knows, why needlessly add to the problem by tinting black all of your windows?

YOUR POINT OF VIEW

How do you get another person
to see your point of view?
Listen very carefully as I tell you exactly
what I think you should do.

First, you should find yourself
just looking all around
For the things that you both agree on
that area called common ground

Also, regardless of who it is
and no matter what the subject
You must always treat your listeners
with the utmost dignity and respect

Make sure that your voice
always has a pleasant tone
If not, they may be turned off
just by this alone

It is also good to remember
that it is always unseasonable
Always, always, the wrong time
for being unreasonable

There is something else
in which there can be no doubt
To get across your point of view
you've got to know what you're talking about

Even when you know your facts
you must still be wary
Never wanting to be condemnatory
Never dogmatic or arbitrary

You should always be gracious
Never rude or crude
But courteous and compassionate
Never displaying a negative attitude

Finally, if your point of view criticizes
Remember this explanation
That when giving counsel or criticism
You always start with commendation

THE BEST IN US-THE WORST IN US: COVID-19

The corona pandemic brought out something in all of us,

The best in us, the worst in us

The best in us was the many, many

doctors, nurses, and other first

responders who came to the aid of the sick and dying

Many of these ones stayed working

24/7 at hospitals and clinics

The worst in us were those who defy the

governmental bans and/or limits put on business,

religious, and social activities

Also, those who shuned p-p-e and "social distancing"

But here was the kicker

"One self styled genius"

offered this as a cure

Gargle with a little bleach or LYSOL

He said: "That will stop the disease for sure"

STOP WHINING, GRIPING, AND CONSTANTLY COMPLAINING

I am tired of hearing people constantly complaining,
griping, whining
Whining about this and whining about that
whining about politicians
The president promised this or he didn't do that
Presidents are politicians and politicians are liars and
Cheaters (that's what they do)
Some do it better than others and so they don't get caught
But they are still politicians and "politicians are all alike
No matter what the color of their stripes"
Republicans, Democrats, Independents, they're all the same
Politicians called by different names.
Politicians are like wolves in sheep's covering
They are out to get you
And they will promise anything to get in office
They cannot fulfill all of those promises
You know this
So stop the complaining

Everybody complains about their job
My job this and my job that
Complaining about one's job seems to be, SOP
People gripe about how many hours they work

How hard they work
They gripe about not getting promoted,
About coworkers and supervisors

Remember, complaining is a lot like frowning
And it takes more energy to frown than to smile
So find something on your job to smile about
And stop the complaining
Blacks complain about whites
The white man this and the white man that
Some blacks blame everything on race
The wife says, "no honey, not tonight, I have a headache"
It's the white man's fault

Junior gets an "F" in Biology
It's the white man's fault

It's true, racism is still alive and kicking in America
But it is not kicking as high as it once did
Still, blacks should never forget their heritage
They should never forget the atrocities
They should never become complacent
But this is a new day
Blacks, you control your own destiny
Blacks, you can now be all that you want to be
And if you don't like the situation
Then do something about it
Only...stop the complaining

Remember Rosa Parks, she wasn't always whining
Martin Luther King didn't sit around complaining
Thurgood Marshall, you didn't hear him always whining
Johnnie Cochran wasn't known for complaining
Again, if you don't like the situation
Then do something about it
Just stop the whining

Some gripe about the police
The police do this and the police do that
They say, "when you don't need them
They're always around
But when you really want them
Not a single one can be found."

When the police shoot the teenager
Who was pointing a gun at them, they gripe
"They didn't have to shoot him so many times"
When they get a ticket for driving 60
In a 25-mile zone, they gripe
"He should have been out catching bank robbers"
Or, "that other car was going faster than I was"
Would you like it if we had no police? No
So stop the complaining

Women gripe about men
Those who don't have a man,
They say all men are dogs
A good man is hard to find
I can do bad by myself

Those who do have a man
My man doesn't do this, or He doesn't do that
He doesn't talk unless he wants sex
Always rough, never gentle

My birthday and our anniversary
He never remembers
He never picks up after himself
What can I do?

You can either train him
Or continue treating him as you would
Like him to treat you
Constantly complaining to your girlfriends
Won't help
So stop the constant complaining

Men gripe about women
Women get on my nerves
They always want to talk
You can't with them and
you can't live without them

I just don't understand women
Why can't they think like men?
They're not supposed to think like men
They're women

And you are not supposed to understand them
They don't understand themselves sometimes
All you have to do is just love them

And be good to them
You want to make your woman happy
And keep her happy?
Pay attention to your woman,
Take notice of her.

Be observant
Notice her hair, her clothes
The expressions on her face
Observe everything about her and around her

Remember these things, comment on them
Talk to your lady
Listen to your lady
Find out the things she likes

Do some of them
Find out what turns her on
And turn her on regularly

Women are like flowers-they want attention
Give it to then and they blossom
So just do it
And stop the constant complaining

Parents whine about their children
"My kids won't do this or they won't do that
These kids just get on my nerves
I need to get away for awhile."

Children act the way they're trained to act
Who trains them? Parents

Either actively or passively
So, if you've got bad kids
You've probably got yourself to blame
So stop the complaining

Children complain about their parents
My parents this or my parents that
They don't understand young people
Too many stupid rules

Young ones, your parents love you
They want the best for you
Your parents are your guardians
Put in charge of you by God
So be obedient to them
Be respectful, God commands this

Remember, youth is not going to last forever
Before you know it you're going to
Be an adult with all of the cares
And worries of adulthood

In the meantime, try to learn as much as you can
And have as much fun as you can
And above all, stop the complaining

Whites complain about blacks
Black people this and black people that
"I'm not a racist," they say,
"but why can't blacks be more like us?"

Why are so many lazy and shiftless?
Why do they always have so many children?
Why do they commit so much crime?
Why do they want to move into our neighborhoods
Lowering out property values?

These things are true of some blacks,
But they are also true of some whites
There is a saying "you reap what you sow"
Whites, you are reaping what you have sown
Blacks were brought here by whites, misused
And abused for 400 years down to this very day

If blacks had been allowed an education long ago
If they had been treated decently and respectfully
Then some of the problems today wouldn't exist
So stop the griping

Finally, if you have a beef with the police
With anybody, with a store, with your whore
Your friend, your lover, your boss, even the
President and you can't meet them face-to-face

Then write them a letter
The keyboard is mightier than the sword
Also, there is something you should always remember
Something you should never forget

And that is…that you are always
A part of the problem
Unless you are part of the solution
So just stop the complaining!

BLACK HISTORY

Black history is filled with great blacks
who did phenomenal things, men and women
Names like Harriet Tubman, George Washington Carver
and Booker T Washington readily come to mind

When our descendants look back on this generation
will they see a multitude of great blacks
who did a multitude of great things?

Or do we today have a disproportionate
number of bay bay kids, of baby daddies and
baby mommas?

Do we still have the drive to strive for greatness?
Do we still believe in dignity and self-respect?
Do we still believe that it takes a village?
Do we still believe that we are our brother's Keepers?
Do we still believe that education is key?
Do we believe that being brainy is not uncool?
Do we believe that being well-dressed, neat and clean
is how we should strive to present ourselves?
Do we believe that being respectful of other people and their
property is an obligation we have?

Well, unless we change some of our thinking
Our black history may very well become
Our black mystery

WHY DIVERSITY?

As I walked down the streets
of Toronto I noticed something
that I am seeing more and more of in
commercial advertisements on American
television
Almost every couple or every family
is biracial
It seems that nobody gets left out anymore
Diversity seems to be the order of the day
Could it be that American business has learned
to accept all people, regardless
of race or color?
Or could it be that this new diversity
has been spawned by so many diverse
folks with so much disposable income?

STOP SEXUAL HARASSMENT

Men with power, men with fame
Do you want to avoid shame and embarrassment?
Then in the workplace, cease and desist
Yes, stop all sexual harassment

Treat all women, younger or older,
As your sister or mother
Treat all men, older or younger
As your father or brother

Always maintain a sense of dignity
Always maintain a sense of class
Never stoop so low as to be
Regarded as a piece off trash

Never make ladies feel uncomfortable
Never make them feel dejected
Always treat them in such a way
That when around you they truly feel respected

So men, keep all your dirty thoughts to yourself
Keep all of your dirty words to yourself
Keep your dirty hands and your dirty lips to yourself
Keep your dirty clothes on your dirty bodies

And above all, keep your dirty power
In your dirty pants

SECTION 9: PUNCTUALITY

What is the meaning of punctuality?
Punctuality's meaning is simple and clear
It means acting or arriving exactly
at the time appointed, not at some time near

PUNCTUALITY

Some folks seem to have an aversion
An aversion to punctuality
Some seem to view it as a sickness
Some kind of abnormality

Being late is bad manners
Being habitually late shows disrespect
It is something that should be avoided
Our being late, others should not come to expect

How does one get out of that habit,
The habit of being late?
Just plan to be on time
Believe it or not, that's all it takes

Here is a good example
If you are due somewhere at nine
And it takes 10 minutes to get there
You must leave before 8:50 to be on time

If you dilly dally all around
And find ways to procrastinate
Thus, leaving AFTER 8:50
Then you will have PLANNED, planned to be late

I HATE BEING LATE

I hate being late, it's bad manners
I hate it when others are late, it's bad manners
I hate it that some like being late
How can I say that some like being late?
The same way that I can say that someone
likes wearing nice clothes.
They always have on nice clothes
Those who like being late are always late
But what about unforeseen occurrences?
Unforeseen occurrences are not what causes
most people to be late
Most are late because they plan to be late!
If they have an appointment at 9 o'clock
they show up at 9:10
If their appointment is at 10 o'clock
they show up at 10:15

They are always late because they plan
to be late
But just as they can plan to be late
they can plan not to be late
But is it reasonable to expect that
everybody is always going to be on time?
Who said anything about being on time?
Don't tell me that there's something
wrong with being on time?

Personally, I don't like being on time!
What can be wrong with being on time?
What can be wrong with being on time
is that you may not have time to get
situated as you would like
So what do you like?

What I like is what solves the problem
What I like is what those who like being late
don't like
What I like is being E-A-R-L-Y
But what about the single mother
with the 12 children?
This is more about the single woman
with no children and no husband
and in good health but always late

BECAUSE HE WAS ALWAYS LATE

He has many fine qualities
But he is always late
Whatever the appointed time
On him you always have to wait

Sometimes it was only a few minutes
other times it is many many more
That he would definitely be late
was the only thing that was sure

"Judgement Day" he was jokingly called
by some of his closest friends
Why? "We know he's coming," they would say
"but only God knows when!

NO SUCH THING AS LATE

When I was in the military there was
no such thing as late
If you were due for an assignment
at 0700 hours and you showed up at 0710
you were not late, you were A-W-O-L,
Absent without leave, a criminal offense
subject to possible jail time

SOME PLAN TO BE LATE

Some folks regard being early as time wasted So they plan to be late Some folks like to make a grand entrance So they plan to be late Some folks care little or nothing about time So they plan to be late Some folks just don't have good manners So they plan to be late Some folks regard being on time as unnecessary So they plan to be late

BEING LATE CAN BE DANGEROUS

Some people in some circles sometimes
say something strange about
those who are habitually late
What do some people in some circles sometimes
say strange about those who
are habitually late?
Some people in some circles sometimes say facetiously
that the person habitually late would
probably be late for his or her own funeral
probably closer to the truth is that
such a person would probably be late
for his or her own salvation

LATE LEAVING LONDON

In 1998, I spent my one-week vacation in
jolly ole London, England.
I revisited places I had been before;
Westminster Abbey, the British Museum,
Trafalgar Square and Piccadilly Circus
to name a few
I literally walked all over London
I also road buses, taxis, as well as
the Underground
My worst experience in London was
when leaving, I was late getting to the airport
For some reason I was shocked that the plane had left without me

ABOUT TIME

Time is like outer space
Time is vast, deep and mysterious
Time we cannot easily define
Time we can best describe
Time has many descriptions
Time is precious
Time marches on
Time flies
Time waits for no one
Time moves forward
Time moves never backward
Time will tell
Time is money
Time is a great healer
Time works wonders
Time, while we cannot define it
Time is a terrible thing to waste

WE ALL HAVE THE SAME AMOUNT OF TIME

There are 24 hours to each day
There are seven days to the week
Thirty days to the month
Thus, we all have the same amount of time
It's how we use our time
That makes the difference

NEVER RUSH WHILE DRIVING

If you wake up late for work
It's okay to rush getting ready
Just never try to make up the time while driving
Unless your vehicle is equipped
With emergency lights and a siren

DON'T ENCOURAGE LATENESS

If you hate lateness then don't encourage it

If you conduct a meeting then always start on time

Start your meeting even if you are the only one there

Never wait for those who love being late For the more you wait,
the more they'll be late

ECCLESIASTES IS NOT WRONG

Ecclesiastes is not wrong in stating
that there is a time and a season for
everything done under the sun
Ecclesiastes is not saying that every person
will have the time in his or her lifetime
to fulfill there every desire
Ecclesiastes is not saying that God presets or predetermines
what happens in our lives
Ecclesiastes is not saying that a person dies
because "their number is up"
Ecclesiastes is not saying that a baby is born
because the clock says it's "birth time"
Ecclesiastes, it must be remembered, it's where it says:
"Time and unforseen occurences befall us all."
Ecclesiastes, in saying that there is a time for
everything means simply that there is an *appropriate*
time for everything
Ecclesiastes means that life and death are both part
of a continuious cycle, with death soon to end

Rev 21:3, 4 KJV

SECTION 10: CHILDREN

Children is the plural of child which
is defined as any person between birth and
puberty. A child is also defined as an
unborn infant; a fetus, infant or baby.
Also, one who is childish, or immature
A child is also the son or daughter or offspring
of two parents. In Biblical usage children
are members of a certain tribe or descendants
Because of being young and inexperienced, children
are special people, people needing guidance
and both tender loving care as well as tough
loving care.
Children are also people, very special people
because children are our future

NEVER PLAY WITH GUNS

If you ever want to have some fun
Then never pick up any kind of gun
A gun is a tool used to kill
Not a toy to give you a thrill
Never point a loaded gun at anyone
Never point an unloaded gun at anyone
Never mimic shooting anyone with a gun

Never point your finger at anyone
and say bang, bang
Again, and again this we say
Never pick up a gun,
Neither real nor play

GOOD MANNERS

Do you have good social behavior?

That is, do you have good manners?

Do you know: "Please, May I, and Thank you"?

Do you hold the door for someone behind you?

Do you come to the aid of someone who suffers a slip, trip or fall?

Do you willlingly share with friends?

Do you offer them the first choice or opportunity?

Do you yell or scream when you disagree with someone?

Do you do good things without having to be asked or told?

THE SCHOOL BUS

When riding on that yellow bus
People are always watching us
So we should always try to be
Both ladylike and mann-er-ly

POLICE AND CROSSING GUARDS

Any act or deed of skill
is sometimes called a feat
What could fit in this category?
It could be crossing a busy street
If there is a policeman or crossing guard
He or she is there for you
Follow their instructions
Do whatever they instruct you to

YOUNG PEOPLE, PLEASE LISTEN AND OBEY

Your parents brought you in this world
They are your guardians, they love you
So, what should you do when they
say what they say when they say
what they say?
Always give them respect, listen and obey

Your teachers are your educators
The lessons of life they help you to learn
so what should you do when they say
what they say when they say what they say?
Always give them respect, listen and obey

The police are your protectors
They help you to keep out of trouble
so what should you do when they say
what they say when they say when they say?
Always give them respect, listen and obey

NAMING CHILDREN

Parents have the right
to name their children
Parents, though, have a duty
to name their children names they can be proud of
Not like the young boy who says
"How do you do? My name is Sue"
But probably worst of all
The dark-skinned Black girl named
Snowball

WAKE UP JUNIOR

Every time he started to snore
we would wake him up and
tell him to go to bed
Each time he would say that he
was not sleep that he was watching TV
Finally, we turned the TV off
and before getting to bed we again
awakened the snorer who again said:
"I'm not sleep, I'm watching TV"

WASH YOURSELF

Each and every morning
or at night
Something you should always do
and do it right
Wash yourself, take a bath
Wash yourself, take a shower

With soap and water
and with a cloth
All of your body parts
wash them off
Arms and legs and in between
All of those places that are never seen
Wash yourself, take a bath
Wash yourself, take a shower

If you do this, what's in store?
All of those loving you will love you more!

THE ICE CREAM MAN

Considered myself being smart
When I went to the super market I
bought a bunch of ice cream novelties-
drumsticks, popsicles, fudgesicles and
creamsicles.
Figured I'd keep my kids from
paying those high prices to the ice cream man
Ring! Ring! Ring!
Ice cream man

Daddy may we have some money
for the ice cream man
There's plenty of ice cream in the freezer
"But we don't want ice cream from the freezer
We want ice cream from the ice cream truck"
After thinking about it for a moment
Thinking back to my youth, I remembered
that it wasn't just the ice cream
Going to the ice cream truck was an event
So I was made to relent

CHILDREN, VERY SPECIAL PEOPLE

Children are not just people
Children are very special people
Children come into the world
With very little knowledge and with
Very few abilities

What children do have is a huge
desire and capacity to learn
From birth they constantly watch,
study and mimic their parents
It was said about Timothy, that
from infancy he had "known the
holy writings,"
so while their baby is still
in the womb some smart mothers
talk to their baby, read to and sing to their baby
To them, children are very special

RESPECT YOUR ELDERS

There is something that I've heard
Something that I've been told
That if you keep waking up everyday
Eventually you're gonna grow old

So while you are young
You should keep yourself in check
Treasure those who have advanced in years
Give them their due honor and respect

Many older ones, from their years of living
Possess a wealth of knowledge
This, some have despite limited formal education
And never having set foot in college

Never degrade or belittle them
Tho' some may be grouchy or a bit too stern
Most though have probably forgotten
More than you will ever learn

Having respect for your elders
Is not just a nice thing to do
Having respect for your elders
Is something that God demands of you

CHILDREN HAVING CHILDREN

Children having children is one of the biggest
contributors to the corruption of today's youth
Children, under 25 are not usually qualified
to raise children
Unlike the farm girl of yesteryear who
got married at 15 who already
had 10 years of experience working on the farm,
working in the field, raising
animals, chicks, pigs, cows and goats-
taking care of the house, washing,
ironing and cooking.
Also, most of life skills by then she would have
acquired
The first 15 years of a child's life
today is spent playing, (mostly video games)
and talking on the phone,
hardly a way to learn any life skills
It used to be that grandparents would
take up the slack, raise the teenager's baby
But many of today's grandparents are too busy
doing their own thing

SOMETHING NICE

Frantically she searched her room
Like the police armed with a warrant
Searching the drawers, tossing it contents
Finally she exclaimed, "it was right here
on my dresser, and now it's gone!

Has anybody seen my diamond bracelet?
Mother, Dad, have you seen my diamond bracelet?
To her younger brother I heard her say
"Donny, come here right away
Have you seen my diamond bracelet?
It was right here on my dresser,
Did you take it?"

She didn't have to ask twice
That look on his face gave him away
What did you do with it?
I took it to school!
For show and tell?, she asked
No, I gave it to Kate

Who is Kate? Kate is my classmate.
Why did you give her my bracelet?
She's pretty, I like her and I wanted
To give her something nice
And I don't have anything nice
How old is this Kate? She's seven just like me

Mother, Dad come here please
Donny gave my bracelet to his girlfriend
Because she's pretty and he wanted o
Give her something nice

Wanting to hear it from him, Mother asked,
"Did you take your sister's bracelet to
school and give it away?"
He opened his mouth and said yes, knowing
That head signals were not permitted

Mother was able to find Kate's mother from
The phone book
Kate brought the bracelet to school and Donny
brought the bracelet back home
Needless to say, Joanne was a happy camper

WATCH HOW YOU WALK

To walk is to move forward by steps
This, most children learn to do
Very early in their childhood
Usually around the age of two

But to walk, boys and girls
truly must learn again
They must learn to walk upright
girls as ladies and boys as gentlemen

OUTSIDE THE SUPERMARKET

Outside the supermarket there were
Some kids hanging around,
5 or 6 of them, perhaps
When they spotted me one of them
strolled over and said:
"Sir, do you have eleven dollars?"
Immediately, I felt my jaw drop
To make sure of what I thought I heard
I looked him squarely in his eyes and said:
"How's that again, son?"
"Do you have eleven dollars," he articulated, again
I didn't lie and say no I don't have
eleven dollars; for I am not one of those
who likes to brag saying: "I never carry cash."
I always carry cash, never leave home without it.
I told him no because in my mind eleven
dollars was too much money to fork over to
some strange kid who just saunters up
to me and ask for it.
I was surprised that he just turned around
and strutted right back over to his crew
I was equally surprised that from the group
a young girl now sashayed over to me
I was more surprised at hearing her words:
"Sir, do you have eleven dollars?
My "No" answer this time was more emphatic

When she turned around and started to
swagger back to her buddies, I then
dashed into the market before they could
send over another crew member.

What they wanted with eleven dollars
I never knew but also what they wanted
with eleven dollars I never cared

A FEW GOOD TABLE MANNERS

One thing you should always do.
Close your mouth when you chew.
Never let your teeth go clack
And never let your lips go smack
At dinner, when it comes to the meat
Cut only one piece at a time to eat
Any kind of talk or conduct
About which you may have some doubt
This would probably be the best time
The very best time to leave it out

THE KIND OF GIRLS BOYS DON'T LIKE

That boys like girls and girls like boys
ain't nothing but the truth
It's just that at certain times
there seems to be not a lot proof
You see, boys don't like:
Girls who are bossy
Girls who are too clingy
Girls who gossip and tattle
Girls who are too nosy
Girls who beat them routinely when
playing games
Girls who hang around when not wanted
Girls who are always putting on airs
Girls who are overly demanding
Girls who don't keep their word
Girls like these, boys don't like

THE KIND OF BOYS GIRLS DON'T LIKE

Boys who treat them as toys, girls don't like

Boys who are sloppy

Boys who don't smell good

Boys who make fun of them

Boys who brag a lot

Boys who are show offs

Boys who disrepect his parents as well as her parents

Boys like these, girls don't like

SECTION 11: POETS, POEMS, AND POETRY

If you were to ask the average person
What a poet is they would probably Say something like, "A poet is one
Who writes and/or recites poetry." In saying
This they would of course be correct because
That is a correct definition of a poet.
However, if you were to ask a poet what
A poet is then he or she would probably
Wax poetic, that is to say, defining a poet Poetically.

WHAT IS A POET?

A poet is one licensed to carry live words, living words
His words, however, should always remain holstered
unless in meter or verse
Not necessarily in rhyme for rhyme has served its time.

Why is the poet granted this license?
It is because language is often very sedate
needing someone to put life into it
To make ordinary speech worth listening to.

How does the poet do this?
On the license it states that he should be gifted in the
perception and expression of the beautiful or lyrical or that
he should have crafted the art of bringing life to language

It further states that he should have mastered comparisons,
handling with ease – similes, metaphors, and personifications.
That he uses them with caution and not with reckless abandon.
The license also numerates other figures of the comparative
type that the poet should have in his arsenal,
namely: synesthesia, synecdoche, epithets,
metonymies, and oxymora.

Anyone well qualified in the aforementioned areas should
have no trouble in being granted a poet's license.

A LITTLE MORE OF THE BEAUTIFUL, PLEASE

To hear beautiful words about beautiful things
Is why I came to the poets den
To hear those beautiful expressions
Written by the poet's pen

I came to hear about the majestic mountains
The mighty oceans and the seven seas
I came to hear about the sun, moon, and stars
About flowers, trees, and leaves

I came to hear about love, joy and peace
About kindness, goodness and self-control
I came to hear about all of the beautiful things
That poets are said to extol

I came not to hear unbridled profanity
I came not to hear wholesale filth and sleaze
And so humbly I ask
A little more of the beautiful, please

"FINISH ME, FINISH ME"

Thousands are those who have one
Because thousands have started one
And so thousands of them cry out:
"finish me, finish me."

Do you have one?
Have you started one?
Do you hear a voice crying out
"finish me, finish me?"

If you have started one
Do you really need to start another?
Or should you be answering that cry,
"finish me, finish me."

Yes, if you have one stashed away
If there is one that heard you say
I'll get back to you some day

Just listen and you'll hear that *manuscript* say
"Finish me, finish me"!

ALMIGHTY GOD LOVES POETRY

Almighty God loves poetry
Poetry Almighty God just loves
And how do we know?
Because the Bible tells us so

Jehovah is a God of culture
Culture abounds with Jah
And just how do we know?
Because the Bible tells us so

Almighty God loves literature,
music, song and dance
Poetry and the arts He also loves
And how do we know?
Because the Bible tells us so

Is there a chapter and verse
saying that God loves poetry?
Is there a chapter and verse
saying that god loves literature and the arts

The answer to both would have to be no
Still the Bible tells us so
Something to consider is this
This is something you might want to consider

The very first person that God created...

was a poet!
For what did Adam do when God presented him
with that beautiful helper that he could
have as a constant companion forever

He broke out with poetry, he waxed poetic, he said:
"This is at last bone of my bones
And flesh of my flesh of my flesh
This one will be called Woman,
Because from man this one was taken."

Was this real poetry?
Of course, it was real!
What is more, it is still real!
But it doesn't rhyme, someone is sure to say
The 23rd Psalm doesn't rhyme but it is one of the
most beautiful poems ever written

Adam's poem is true in form
with an economy of words,
each phrase nicely matching the next,
with a progression of thought
and perfect balance
From where did Adam get this poetic prowess?
He got it from his poetry loving God
and Father in whose image he was created
Not that he looked like God, but that he
possessed some of the qualities and
attributes of God – one in particular –
the ability to put beautiful words together
in a beautiful way

So how do you think God felt about
that poetry and that poet?
God loved that poet and his poetry
Appointed him Poet Laureate of the
Garden of Eden
Lamech who lived around Adam's time
wrote poems to his two wives
The scriptures literally abound with poetry

Especially, the Psalms, Proverbs,
The Song of Solomon and Lamentations

Many of those used by God in writing
the Scriptures were poets
Moses, David, Solomon, and Jeremiah to name a few

That Almighty God loves poetry
How do we know?
Because the Bible tells us so!

NEITHER A COMEDY NOR DIVINE

There once was an Italian author considered to be
one of the greatest poets of the middle ages
An epic "comedy" of his ranks among the finest works
of world literature.
Critics have praised it not only as magnificent poetry
but also, for its "wisdom" and "scholarly learning"
Scholars revered this poem so much that they
dubbed it "divine."
The poem had a tremendous influence on many
later writers from Chaucer to Shelly
The poem has one very, very big flaw, however
After further review, the poem proves to be
not "divine" but also not a "comedy"
A more apt description would be a "collection of errors"
And now for the errors

The teaching or belief that we are somehow
still alive after death is an error
The teaching that all good people go
to heaven for a life of bliss is an error
The belief that the wicked burn in a
hellish inferno after death is an error
The belief that those who were not good
enough to go straight to heaven get their souls
purged with fire in a place called
purgatory located on the edge of hell; A big error

The belief that hell is the home of the Devil and
his demons is an error
The belief that beliefs based on errors
could be divine is itself an error

All of these errors preclude the poem
from being a comedy, from having a true
happy ending
Fraught with so many errors also prevents it
from being divine
For the divine teaching about death is clear:
"The living know that they are going to die
but the dead know not anything" – Eccl 9:5 KJV
"The soul that is sinning, it itself will die" – Ezk 18:4

GIVE ME A TITLE, PLEASE!

Some poets sometimes say something strange
about poem titles
What do some poets sometimes say strange
about poem titles?
Some poets sometimes say that they
don't care for titles – that a title
is too much of a commitment
I am a poet, what do I say?
I say; "Give me a title, please!"
I say that a title is indeed a commitment-
a commitment promising a payoff
If I, the audience will invest my time
and effort to read or listen to your work
and there is no title, how will I not feel
shortchanged?
If there is no title, how will I know
the gist of what the poem is supposed to be saying?
If there is no title, how powerful
Can the poem be?
If there is no title, how can I know
whether the poem is any good or not
so I say again; "Give me a title, please!"

WHAT IS POETRY?

What is poetry?
Poetry is literature
But not just any piece of literature

Poetry is any piece of literature
Written in measured rhythm
That is to say, in meter

Poetry is any piece of literature
Written prosodically
That is to say, in verse

Poetry is any piece of literautre
Where certain words are found
At the end or middle, words that
Are different, but have the same sound
That is to say, they rhyme

Poetry is any piece of literature
Not falling victim to the curse
Any piece of literature not tightly
bound by Rhythm, rhyme or verse
That is to say, free verse

THE "F" BOMB (#$@&%*!)

Just as Hollywood movie makers once put
a cigarette between the lips of
all of its stars
Today's profanatory movie makers have the
"F" word coming from the mouths
of sweet little old ladies, from priests,
nuns, and even little children
One 2013 blockbuster dropped the
"F" bomb more than 500 times
And just as many folks, imitating the stars,
began using cigarettes so likewise,
many have now made the "F" word a
big part of their vocabulary
Sad to say, there are some poets who seem
to think the "F" bomb is some kind of
integral poetic device that they must
explode in their every poem

MY GRANDDAUGHTER'S BAPTISM- I WAS ELATED!

I was elated when I was invited
to my granddaughters baptism.
I received the invitation well in advance
and like the special occasion it was,
I circled it on the calender; November 16th 2019.
Not only did I circle it but I also marked off the days.
I was elated because of what her baptism meant.
It meant that at the tender age of 15, that Avi, my favorite
granddaughter had in prayer to God dedicated her life to him.
I was even more elated when she came up out of the water.
I was elated then and I am elated now.

PROVERBS

A Proverb is a brief saying that presents a truth or some bit of useful wisdom. It is usually based on common sense or practical experience. The effect of a proverb is to make the wisdom it tells seem to be self evident. Many proverbial sayings employ likenesses or comparisons. Kings and other rulers have been known for uttering proverbs. However, the most noteable collection of such sayings are found in the Bible, in the Book of Proverbs.

●

Sometimes the best way to show
how smart you are is to show how mum you can be.

●

Merely being still above ground
means not a lot if you have little or no quality of life.

●

Young children need discipline.
Talking is good most times.
Sometimes, sometimes, belt on butt is best

●

Just like "everybody talking about
heaven ain't going to heaven," so
likewise, everybody talking about
they're blessed ain't blessed!

LIMERICKS

A limerick is a five line form of humorous verse.
It is written in poulter's measure, which consists
of 13 beats and has a rhyme scheme of aa bb a.
Limericks are most often off color and so most
are off limits to me.

There was a young lady from Zin
Who was so exceedingly thin
That when looking at her from the side
You would think she was trying to hide
For with her surroundings she blended in

What nation once had as its leader
One viewed as the world's biggest liar and cheater
Who was highly uncouth and brazenly brash
Viewed by many as mere big city trash
A dishonest and corrupt repeater

Ministers molesting boys is not new
It's something they always used to do
Now their church is having to pay
For using men who were obviously gay
Because everybody is now trying to sue

Our church once hired a pastor
Who was a complete disaster
For he had a rap sheet
That was almost three feet
And growing faster and faster

The man was obsessed
Always saying "I'm blessed"
Until it was found
That in mind he was not sound
For being a serial killer he confessed

Want to stop rioting and looting?
Then stop the senseless killing and shooting
Demand that the police keep themselves in check
That they treat everyone with the utmost dignity and respect
Lest they suffer a sure and swift booting

People were always making quips
About Suzie's ultra big hips
Until one day She got in a fray
Punching someone right in their lips

HAIKU

The Japanese celebrate their land and people with what is known as haiku; a three-line non-rhyming form of poetry. Starting out, haiku was part of a 31 syllable, five-line verse form called waka or tanka. By the Middle Ages, aspiring poets found joy in using waka in a sort of literary game; one giving the first three lines and another matching them with two more. In time, the opening three-line form became popular on it's own, and thus giving birth to the haiku. Today's haiku is a lesson in brevity. The first and last lines are five syllables each, while the middle one is seven. Haiku usually deals with some subject in nature. The rules for haiku are not always hard and fast, especially the 5-7-5 rule. For example, a haiku by Japanese poet Issa, when translated has two lines of 10 syllables each. Others have any number of syllables per line. Basho, likewise doesn't always follow the rules.

Haiku #1 The Death Of Death

Haiku #2: Hell's Death

Death's days are numbered
Hell's days are also numbered
Both are soon to die

Hell's death is coming
Soon says the Revelation
Twenty Verse fourteen

-KJV

Haiku #3 Old Age And Death

Haiku #4 We All Go

Growing old and death
Two of the most dreadful things
Two terrible times

Hell is but the grave
Everybody who dies
They all go to hell

Haiku #5 Death Not Intended

To live forever
To die, never no never
That's how God made us

Haiku #6 Resurrection From Hell

The Revelation
Describes the resurrection
of all those from hell

Haiku #7 Whole Bible Needed

Half of the Bible
Will not give you the whole truth
Old Testament too

Haiku #8 Prayed To Go To Hell

Prayed to go to hell
Who requested such a thing?
It was the man Job

Haiku #9 The Dead Know Nothing

That they will taste death
The living know they will die
The dead know nothing

Haiku #10 The Death Of Hell

Death and hell will end
After the resurrection
says Revelation

Haiku #11 Hell Is Not Hot

Not as hot as hell
The Bible hell is not hot
Jesus went to hell

Haiku #12 The Enemy

Death is not our friend
Death is our great enemy
No one sane wants death

ABOUT THE POET

Luther Whitley is a native Washingtonian and was educated in the D.C. Public School System. A voracious reader and serious student of the Scriptures, he spent many years in his church ministries, especially in speaking and teaching. Writing Bible discourses, songs and poems, as well as attending writing seminars helped him to develop his writing skills. It was his eighth grade English teacher he says who excited his interest in poetry. There were two poems that he fell in love with and immediately committed to memory. They were *Thanatopsis* by William Cullen Bryant and *The Raven* by Poe.

Whitley says that he has read and studied many of the great poets of the world. He is especially fond of those whose writing style is similar to his, those noted for the use of everyday dialect as well as free verse. Whitley has read and has been the featured poet at venues all around Washington, D.C. This list includes Howard University, Martin Luther King Jr library, SW Library, NE Library, Oxon Hill Library, Bowie Library, Largo/Kettering Library, just to name a few.

Whitley's books include *The Truth About Capital Punishment* and *Thou Shall Not Kill, Christmas – The Lie That Everybody Loves, Proverbial Sayings of an Ordinary Man, The Plight of the Honey Bee* and other poems; *The Spectacular Rise and Foretold Fall of Christianity* and *My 69 Trilogies–Poems in Groups of Threes.*

Printed in the United States
By Bookmasters